When I Listen

words and art by
Oshri Liron Hakak

BUTTERFLYON BOOKS

First Edition
Copyright ©2024, by Oshri Liron Hakak
All Rights Reserved

When I Listen
Art and Words by Oshri Liron Hakak

Published by Butterflyon Books
Los Angeles
ISBN 979-8-9868755-8-3

In loving remembrance of Thich Nhat Hanh,
and to listeners…
May we grow and deepen in our listening.

When I listen,
I listen with the quietness of a stone,
who is stable, steady, and solid
in its silent stillness.

When I listen,
I listen with the patience of a lichen,
who slowly and surely brings life
to barren desert rocks.

When I listen,
I listen with the rootedness of a tree,
whose branches can wave in the wind
even while the tree stays calm in its center,
and who can stand strong
for thousands of years,
growing leaf by leaf
and twig by twig.

When I listen,
I listen with the faith of a momma bird
nudging her fledgling on its first flight,
knowing that this is how it will learn
to use its wings.

When I listen,
I listen with the big, open ears
of an elephant,
who hears all the high sounds
and all the low sounds,
big and small,
even from great distances.

When I listen,
I listen with the truthfulness of a lake,
reflecting perfectly from where it sits.

When I listen,
I listen with the ease of a duck,
who fluffily, featherfully floats on the water
without getting its skin wet.

When I listen,
I listen with the deep and silent sounds
of a whale
who bathes all life of the sea
in gentle and loving vibrations
that nourish creatures
even when they don't hear them.

When I listen,
I listen with the sweetness of a puppy,
whose gentle, fuzzy cuddliness
always leaves room for paws.

When I listen,
I listen with the heart-softening faith of a flower,
who trusts in the wind
and in its connection with many creatures
to carry its future.

When I listen,
I listen with the goodwill of a bee,
who gathers nectar
and shares its own sweetness
by spreading pollen from flower to flower,
supporting all kinds of life
all around the planet, hour to hour.

When I listen,
I listen with the depth of a mycelial mushroom,
who connects and supports life
through its huge (several square miles),
underground web
that no one sees.

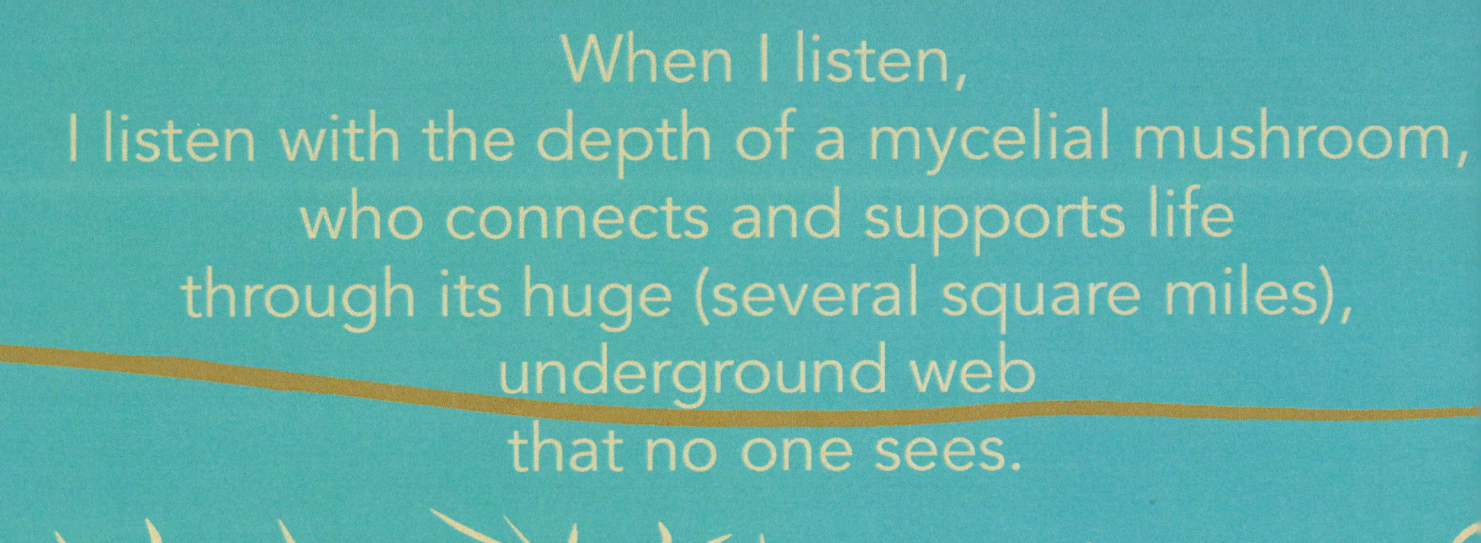

When I listen,
I listen with the playfulness of a panda,
who knows that it takes playfulness
to be serious,
that we can often serve life by being
lighthearted, joyful and curious.

When I listen,
I listen with the solidness of a mountain,
on whose slopes and surroundings
life takes root and abounds,
generation after generation.

When I listen,
I listen with the openness of the sky,
which our eyes created
to make sense of the reality
that any direction we look up
is a space of infinity.

When I listen,
I listen with the mystery of the moon,
whose regular disappearance and return
gives us courage to explore and come back
from our own dark places.

When I listen,
I listen with the generosity of the sun,
bursting for billions of years
with warmth and light,
feeding life and growth on earth,
allowing for our gift of sight.

When I listen,
I listen with the spaciousness of the cosmos,
so vast that they contain all experiences
and all perspectives for all time,
not tiring from repetition,
nor ever feeling worried about change
or competition.

When I listen,
I listen with the love of a parent
putting a child to sleep,
a moment that life holds most tender,
powerful and deep…
for it whispers through the ages:
"As you close your eyes and rest, My Dear,
you are safe, you are loved,
and always will I be near."

(bl)end

(of all life into harmony and oneness)

A Listening Practice: Listen Within

As you are sitting comfortably with your eyes closed, or as you are drifting off to sleep, gently slow your breathing down…

Place your awareness on all the sounds you are experiencing. Focus especially on the sounds coming from inside of you. You may hear the sound of your breath, or of the beat of your heart, or the sounds of all the oceanic activity of your brain.

Consciously match the sound of your breath with your inner sound.

Allow your breath to slow and deepen, letting your body relax.

Gratitude

Thank you Allan Vogel, for inspiring the inner listening practice at the end of this book.

Thank you to my friends and family, for listening to me.

Thank you, Earth, for singing to me.

Thank You NAMI Westside Los Angeles

Thank you to NAMI Westside Los Angeles for supporting the creation of this book. NAMI Westside Los Angeles is a part of NAMI, a grassroots mental health advocacy organization that offers free education, programming and support for people who are struggling with mental health conditions, as well as for those who are supporting loved ones experiencing challenging mental health conditions.

Mental health for anyone is good for everyone. No matter who you are and where you are, you are not alone. You can find out more about NAMI and its offerings at NAMIWLA.org.

About the Author

Oshri loves to make art, music and books to aid people and communities in our individual and collective healing journey.

You can find more of Oshri's books on ButterflyonBooks.com . His art and music are on instagram—@oshrihakak .